It's All About the Love

Surviving, Thriving, and Understanding Life's Losses

It's All About the Love

Surviving, Thriving, and Understanding Life's Losses

Cheryl Cuttineau

Happy At Home Publishing

Cover design: Jacob Brooks Fiegle, artbyjbrooks.myportfolio.com

Published by Happy at Home Publishing

Note:
This is a work of non-fiction. These are real events.
However, some names have been changed.

First Edition: September 2024

10 9 8 7 6 5 4 3 2 1

ISBN: 978-1-83556-193-5

From the Author--

Thank you so much for your interest in my book. My story is a bit of an adventure, so I hope you enjoy the ride.

May I ask you for a favor?

As a beginning book publisher, it would mean a lot to me if you would consider leaving an honest review on Amazon.com. It doesn't have to be elaborate. Just share your thoughts about whether the book helped you or not. If so, how?

Constructive reviews from wonderful readers like yourself help other readers feel confident about choosing a book. It also helps me improve the quality of future books, so sharing your experience is greatly appreciated.

Thank you again for your interest in *It's All About the Love.* I hope it earns your trust and encourages you to read other new authors.

Blessings,

Cheryl Cuttineau

Happy At Home Publishing
Laguna Beach, California

TABLE OF CONTENTS

PROLOGUE

IT HAS BEEN SAID THAT MANY FAMILIES are only one paycheck from disaster and being homeless.

What happened to me can happen to anyone. A friend or colleague. Your loved ones or relatives. Your spouse.

Even You.

There were signs. Some people call them "whispers" from the universe that grow louder if we don't listen or pay attention.

I was living in my dream home in my dream community. I started my new business freelancing as a writer. I adopted three sibling kitties who provided endless hours of laughter and delight. It was the happiest time of my life.

And then it was all gone. The dream, the lifestyle, the business, the money, even the kitties.

Gone.

Life does, and can, turn on a dime.

DEDICATION

I DEDICATE THIS WORK TO THOSE WHO have suffered a traumatic loss of any kind and survived to tell about it: a miscarriage or the death of a child, the death of a spouse, a divorce, bankruptcy, loss of a home, a business failure, a devastating medical diagnosis, or even the death of a beloved pet.

This is also a tribute to the untold thousands who wake up each day on the streets, in shelters, or in their cars, holding onto hope for a better future and a place to call their own, instead of being lost in their circumstances.

Never stop searching. Never give up.

Help is closer than you think. The restoration you seek may be in the face of an angel disguised as a stranger you meet.

Or, like Dorothy in The Wizard of Oz, the solutions may be found within yourself.

ACKNOWLEDGEMENTS

TO ALL THE FRIENDS WHO ALLOWED ME to inconvenience their lives and couch-camp in their living room or sleep in their spare bedroom.

To the Goddess Brigade—an eclectic group of powerful women of kindness, generosity and strength. Collectively and individually, you were a life support of caring, help, and financial support. In alphabetical order, I honor you: Carole, Cindy, Collette, Diana, Gretchen, Isabella, Jeannine, Jenny, Kathleen, Milly, Peggy, Rachel, Sena Rose, Sharla, and Vanessa.

To Rev. Sandy, Rev. Kirk and In Spirit CSL—for your unwavering support and an interesting place to sleep and work in "the Upper Room" at the Do Drop Inn (!)

To Michael—My Forever Best Friend.

To Aida Hobbs—for your friendship, ceaseless encouragement, and welcoming home sanctuary between gigs.

To Petra Sovella-Farber, Medicine Woman—for your friendship, support, and Wise Women's Book Circle every Thursday.

To Sue & Jeff Kouba—for your kindness and generosity.

To Barbara Carr—for your friendship and generous gift of healing.

To Suzanne Taylor—my first safe refuge, and "Blacky."

To Angenieta L—Thank you for your friendship and support. "Arm in arm!"

To Michael W—Thank you for the wonderful opportunity to work with you and your staff.

To Tammy & Dave D—6 months turned into 2 ½ years! You inspired the title!

To Cris and Dan—Thank you for sharing your home during the Pandemic and post-pandemic!

To Ronn Sarno and Joannie Neumann—the most I have laughed on any Christmas Decorating Committee!

To all my pet sitting clients. Your fur babies filled the hole in my soul over the loss of my little tribe and kept away the emptiness in my heart: Bear; Annie Cat & Molly, Bandit & Ranger; Gunner; Greta Joy; Annie; Blacky; Jackson; Mortimer & Agatha; Zoey, Sasha & Abigail; Stitch & Ginger; Smokey Bear & Little Bear; Beau, Riley & Carlos; Ivan, Sea-C & Lilly; Mandy, Kingsley & Molly; Lucy/Lucchia; Zeva, Abigail, Patches, Punkin, Scooter & Daisy; Bella, Asha & Domino; Max & Genie; Dandy & Domino; Story, Rusty &

Mikey; all the homeless cats and dogs awaiting adoption at Best Friends No-Kill Adoption Center in West Los Angeles; Dexter, Little, Nell, and the family of raccoons.

I am grateful to the Laguna Woods Cat Club for their financial support in taking care of my cats when I couldn't keep them.

Many thanks to Members of the Laguna Niguel Library Writer's Club who provided honest criticism, feedback, and encouragement.

To Agape International Spiritual Center, Rickie Byars, Rev. Coco, and Dr. Rev. Michael Beckwith—your community uplifted my spirit, and your music healed this broken heart.

Much love and gratitude to Rickie Byars and Dr. Rev. Michael Beckwith for their kind and generous permission to reprint excerpts from songs they co-wrote that were pivotal in my journey.

FORWARD

By Susan Robertson, RSP
Center for Spiritual Living
Mission Viejo, California

November 27, 2022

THERE ARE MANY POSITIVE WAYS TO manage life during difficult times of crisis, confusion, and chaos. Since most changes can bring about stress, it is important for our mental and physical health to acknowledge the stress and re-channel that energy to focus on positive ways of navigating life and developing resilience.

We can practice optimistic self-talk. As we notice our thoughts and patterns, we can challenge and change our thinking. We can swap out negative thinking for more positive, optimistic thoughts and see the good in every situation. We can start thinking about a new life plan and revise our desires and visions, finances, or future activities.

Resilience can be described as a "person's capacity to cope with changes and challenges and to bounce back during difficult times." Resilience is composed of multiple factors, including social support, self-care behaviors, and cognitive flexibility.

Something important to remember is that anyone can be resilient. It is not strictly a skill we are born with or a natural quality that we have; it is a combination of skills, strategies, and environmental factors that can be developed over time. We can KNOW we will be ok, we are one with God, and we are NOT alone.

Instead of feeling the anxiety of the unknown, we can trust that "this, too, shall pass" and we will get through the situation at hand peacefully and calmly. Pema Chodron says, "To be fully alive, fully human, and completely awake is to be continually thrown out of the nest." If we are up against a wall, if we have suffered loss or experienced grief, we can move toward hope and faith as we transform our most difficult situations into opportunities for growth and expansion.

Research has shown that individuals who demonstrate resilience are more adept at recovering from "experiences of adversity and trauma." Resilient individuals are better able to deal with everyday stress, and often experience more positive health outcomes and statistically have lower rates of anxiety and depression.

Resilience is about adaptability and adjustment—getting back up despite being knocked down. It is vital to remember that, as humans, we will be challenged by the difficulties and stress that life throws at us.

However, if we develop skills like resilience, we can learn more effective ways of managing those challenges and navigate life from a more powerful perspective.

CELEBRITIES WHO HAVE BEEN HOMELESS

- Debbie Reynolds
- Colonel Sanders
- Iyanla Van Zant
- Sarah Van Breathnach
- Jennifer Lopez
- Jean-Claude Van Damme
- Tyler Perry
- Steve Harvey
- Hilary Swank
- Drew Carey
- Halle Berry
- Suze Orman
- Shania Twain
- Jim Carrey
- Kelly Clarkson
- Sylvester Stallone
- Steve Jobs
- Dr. Phil McGraw

INTRODUCTION

IT WAS MAY 7, 2014, AND MY ENTIRE LIFE and everything I had come to understand had flipped upside down and inside out.

I brought my last two adopted kitties, Billy Ray and Farrah, to the cat boarding service supported by a local rescue organization. The new "kitten adoption season" had not yet swung into full operation. This meant my one-year-old cats had a higher chance of finding foster or temporary homes until they could be adopted. Much to my relief, Heather, the smallest female sibling, had already been placed in foster care until she could be adopted.

As Billy Ray and Farrah settled into a large cage with an oversized bed, I noticed Billy Ray's gigantic eyes staring over the side of the bed while he tried to conceal himself. Farrah cowered behind him, too terrified to look at the strange surroundings.

I tearfully said goodbye to them and cried all the way back to the condo. I no sooner pulled into the driveway than I received a phone call from a friend and fellow cat rescue volunteer. Aware of the circumstances, she called to console me. But I was too distraught and sobbed uncontrollably through our conversation. When I first brought them to my home, the sibling kittens were only eight weeks old. I had made a solemn vow I would take care of them all the rest of their days. Now I had failed them. Relinquishing ownership of all three cats was the hardest thing I had ever done.

After our phone call ended and I got control of myself, I packed up my car for the last time with all the clothes and personal items I would need for the journey ahead. I took one more walk through my dream home, said goodbye for the last time, and left the house keys on the kitchen counter.

I will never forget Billy Ray's enormous eyes, so full of fear and confusion. He stared out at the unknown, his eyes large with terror. Like a mirror, he showed me my own fear and uncertainty. At least I knew he and Farrah and Heather would be taken care of.

I was not as certain about my future.

# # # # #

A Roadmap For The Reader:

This book is organized just like my seven-year journey: circuitous. Stop and go. Dead ends and rabbit holes. If you are expecting a linear A-to-Z experience, sorry to disappoint you; but if we are being very honest, life is not like that. Life lived in harmony with Nature is like a stream. It has its ebbs and flows, currents that stall or bolt. Obstacles may block its way until the stream either wears down the obstacle over time or finds a way around it.

Through my experience, I realized there are two ways to live life: one way symbolized by a sailboat that follows the current and allows life events to happen; the other way symbolized by a locomotive heading full throttle on a train track. I was very much the locomotive with the "be in control and make life happen" mentality. The truth was, I was anything but in control. My locomotive was speeding towards the edge of a cliff, and my life was about to get REAL interesting.

THE LESSONS

So let's jump in on one of the detours.

The big message of this book is that you can survive and thrive in any crisis involving loss, IF you really want to.

Yes, You CAN.

Think about the countless number of Holocaust survivors who endured unspeakable horrors and witnessed man's savage cruelty to his fellow man.

Reflect on the war hostages held in North Vietnamese prison camps who were beaten and tortured daily under horrific conditions for years. The ones who survived made it through to the day they were released from prison.

Indigenous peoples from the Native Americans to victims of the slave trade were kidnapped and removed from their homes and lands. Wounded Knee and "the trail of tears" are testimony to man's inhumanity to man. The survivors somehow endured.

What these groups had in common was the mindset to survive. The mindset that included resiliency in the face of deepest sorrow and loss.

Yes, you can survive tragedy and loss, but you must be armed with certain beliefs and mindset.

You may never suffer the loss and tragedy of a holocaust. However, when loss and tragedy suddenly strike, the pain can feel just as hurtful.

Below are some of the "lessons" that I learned during my experience. Briefly, they are:

1. Accept that we are not in control of everything.
2. Learn to be content and make peace with all things and situations.
3. Be Grateful. For anything. Practice being in gratitude. No matter how crummy circumstances appear. Things can always be worse!
4. Ask for help and be grateful for whatever or whomever shows up.
5. Beware: the road to hell is paved with good intentions.
6. Learn to recognize and trust your intuition.
7. Learn to identify external clues and signs from the Universe.
8. We are 100% responsible for our own happiness.
9. Don't take anything personally.

10. Never, EVER give up.

I learned these lessons the hard way, through experience. I would never understand on a deep level what these meant had I not gone through the actual seven years. No book, no seminar, no workshop could teach me what I learned and integrated deep into my soul. Behind the tears, the heartbreak, the grief and the deep night of the soul, there were unseen forces surrounding me and guiding me every step of the way.

These became my lessons for survival and learning to overcome obstacles by going through them. More than that, the revelations, insights and understanding became ways to share with anyone who faces similar circumstances and perhaps give them Hope.

PREFACE

"Early in the morning laying in my bed
Thinking about a dream I had
Pictures were fading fast
Noticing the music in each scene
And a peace beyond this world
I recalled
That I couldn't dwell in what was wrong
Couldn't care about what had gone
The message on the stereo was strong
Saying Lord, let the pain go
And one day we see
Is what really matters in life or in dreams
Is the music of Love we hear in each scene."

Excerpt from "I'm Ready to Listen," composed by Rickie Byars and Michael Beckwith and reprinted here with kind permission from Eternal Dance Music, BMI ©2000.

Chapter One

"When God is moving you toward a new awareness,
You need to recognize the winds of change at once
And move with them instead of clinging
To what is already gone."
--Marion Woodman (1928-2018)

WHEN WE LIVE COMFORTABLE LIVES we cannot fathom living any other way. I lived like that for two-thirds of my life.

But there are thousands of men and women who live in the shadows, many of them homeless. If they are lucky, they live out of a car each day and night. They must take care of hygiene day by day. Where to get money to buy food or gas. Staying below the radar and avoiding the tow truck if they are behind on car payments. Dealing with depression and despair, hoping to find some miracle "traction" and stability on which to stand.

Early in my journey, I was desperate to seek out people who had experienced and survived a similar crisis. Iyanla Van Zant and her book, *Peace from Broken Pieces,* were pillars I clung to, especially in the early days when I suffered the most. I had to know that I was not alone, that my experience was not an isolated case, and that there was a way out.

I was fortunate to have a laptop computer and access to the Internet at the local library. I found lists of well-known celebrities who had been homeless to convince myself I just wasn't the loser I felt I was. I would search for videos of uplifting, inspiring, and motivational speakers. It became a habit to listen to these winners rather than cry myself to sleep, which I did, nightly, early in my experience.

Iyanla Van Zant was always my favorite, and I would often fall asleep listening to one of her talks. She had been to hell and back and knew what REAL loss was about. She survived and thrived. Nearly everything that she lost was returned to her, just like the story of Job in the Bible. She will say it wasn't easy, and things did not turn around overnight, but she did the work and put her life back together, piece by piece.

Lesson Number 7 says to learn to identify external clues and signposts from the Universe. One day I stopped in a Michael's Craft Store. I didn't have a lot of money but I felt the need to find something beautiful to remind me that I still had something beautiful in my life. I found a small inexpensive glass lotus that was just perfect! I was so excited about my purchase that I dropped the wrapped item on the sidewalk. When I carefully unwrapped the paper, to my dismay, the figure was broken into several pieces. I seriously considered going back to the store to get a new one.

But the message, the "whisper," behind the broken pieces did not escape me. I kept my new symbolic treasure to remind me I, too, was rebuilding my NEW life, piece by piece.

And I still have that glass lotus, encircled by its broken pieces.

It is one of my most treasured possessions!

Chapter Two

2013: THE YEAR FROM HELL

SO WHAT HAPPENED TO ME? HOW DID I transition from living in my dream home with a six-figure salary to living in my car or couch-surfing for almost seven years?

2013 was the worst year of my life. I cherished my home and refuge from the outside world, but circumstances in the shape of a "perfect storm" had begun to close in on me. Beginning with the loss of long-time animal companions, my calico cat Molly, 24, and her daughter Coco, 22, succumbed to old age within 4 months of each other. Animals come into our lives for a reason or a season, and Molly and Coco accompanied me through the most tumultuous years of my life yet. They had fulfilled whatever unseen agreement they may have had with me, and now it was their time to move on.

A Week In The Life of A Teacher

After 14 years, I came to hate public education. Working conditions went from bad to worse, and then the district eliminated the Independent Studies program I was in. The district assigned me to work at two different school sites an hour's drive from each other. I already commuted 100 miles each way from my home.

Every week, I gathered teacher edition textbooks, student files, corrected assignments, and office supplies and transported them to the first school site for the first two days of the week. Once I arrived at 7am, I unloaded the car and took everything into the "office space" (previously a storage room) to prepare for my 8am meeting with my first student.

Once school ended on the second day, I packed up my car for the long journey home. For the rest of the week, I drove an hour further to the second school site to repeat the process: arrive by 7 am, set up my "office" which was now the utility room housing the school alarm system and electrical circuitry, and prepare to meet with my first student at 8am.

Hardly ideal conditions for mentoring students and helping them improve their work habits.

At the end of the week, I assembled all my textbooks, student files, assignments, and office supplies, loaded them into the trunk of my car, and headed for home. Depending on the traffic, the drive sometimes took up to two hours.

Why Did I Stay?

The Independent Studies program in my district was a safety net for those middle and high school students who could not participate in the general school curriculum or school population. Victims of bullying or sexual assault, drugs, gang activity, juvenile hall or criminal offenders were all candidates for this program. Some advanced students enrolled in Independent Studies to accelerate academically and graduate early. Students met with a teacher each week and received individualized studies that followed district guidelines.

In the Fall of 2012, the district informed the four Independent Studies teachers that the program was ineffective and we would be assigned to different schools. During the Spring of 2013, without any input or feedback from me, I was re-assigned to one of the least popular curriculums and the worst school in the district, academically and behavior-wise. The reassignment would take place the new Fall Semester of 2013. Imagine the challenge of teaching the California State Education standards for 9th Grade on *Romeo and Juliet* to adolescent students who struggle with English language skills, reading below a 5th-grade level, or possibly unable to read, write, or speak English at all.

I could not begin to reckon my state of mind if I allowed myself to be abused any further.

I made several attempts to obtain teaching positions at a local charter school closer to my home. I even received two offers of employment, but in the public education profession, educators are contractually bound to an annual contract. Unlike other professions, we can't give two weeks' notice and leave.

If I were to break my contract with the district, there would be legal consequences, not to mention a suspension of my state teaching credential. The district may, at its discretion, release a teacher from the contract. My district refused my request both times.

I felt trapped. That's when the physical ailments began.

The Body Expresses What the Emotions Cannot

By the end of January 2013, I began to have physical issues. By the end of February, I had full-blown plantar fasciitis and tendonitis in both feet. "The emotion that cannot find its expression in tears may cause other organs to weep" (Dr. Henry Maudsley,1835-1918).

I originally objected to going on disability due to the reduction in pay AND the daily deduction to pay for a substitute teacher (whether one was hired or not). My supervisor noticed all the sick hours I was taking and directed me to go on disability leave. Driving a car in my condition was especially dangerous, so going on leave was a blessing in disguise. I was not present at school from March through the end of May.

I would have stayed out the rest of the school term, but I wanted to close out my student grade books and submit final grades. I had already decided to resign in June.

But a rude surprise awaited me. In another black eye for academic integrity, the retired, highly respected veteran English teacher who had been hired to fill in for me had altered my earlier grades. Previously failing students who turned in incomplete assignments, plagiarized work, or turned in nothing at all were suddenly receiving grades of A in all subjects, with no student work to substantiate the changes.

Wasn't that sweet of her?

Unbeknownst to anyone, before I went on leave, I made copies of my grade sheets and had a record of all the percentages of work that had been corrected by me through the end of February.

I ended up having to re-do all the grade sheets that had been snow-paked by this other teacher. I also had to conference with those students whose grades had been fraudulently inflated. On the day for final grades to be submitted, I took several student files to the supervisor's office and left the final grades incomplete and unsigned. I included a letter about the academic fraud, the changing of my grades by the other teacher, and my refusal to sign off on any of the work.

On June 6, 2013 (6-6-6), I walked into the district office and turned in my letter of resignation. I happily walked away from the most frustrating, punishing, soul-sucking experience of my life. I collected my pension in one lump sum and paid off all my debts. Then I adopted three orphaned kittens.

Second Thoughts

Did I do the right thing by leaving my 6-figure job without having another job lined up? Had I been too rash and foolishly put myself in harm's way?

Something strange happened on the way home from work one Friday evening that confirmed there was no turning back, come what may.

I was still employed by the school district. On my first week back from being on disability leave, I was distressed that the other teacher had changed my grades. More like angry. I was driving home on the Ortega Highway, leaving Lake Elsinore. I drove uphill against traffic so that the cars on my side were few and far between. But the opposite lane, with traffic backed up and stopped around the blind curves and twisting highway, was a disaster waiting to happen.

The Ortega Highway is a narrow two-lane highway. The downhill lane coming from Orange County into Riverside County hugs the hills and landscape. The uphill lane leaving Riverside County in the direction of Orange County is on the side of a cliff. The portion of the highway overlooking Lake Elsinore is very scenic, but take your eyes off the narrow road at your own peril.

There were two white Mercedes SUVs ahead of me and a late model sedan behind me. There was little traffic in my lane as I drove leisurely up the hillside. I reached a part of the highway where there was a blind curve on the other side. Drivers coming down the hillside would not be able to see the stalled traffic around the curve and stop in time.

A white pickup truck was traveling too fast down the hill in the other lane. When the driver suddenly saw the stopped cars in his lane, he sharply veered to the left and crossed the center divider into oncoming traffic. His truck spun out of control and side-swiped both SUVs ahead of me.

The truck continued to spin and careened towards me.

There was no place to escape. I was trapped between two cars, one in front and one behind me, and to my right was the sheer, steep side of the cliff.

I Will Never Forget What Happened Next For As Long As I Live

The next few moments were surreal. I remember thinking, "Well, this is where my life ends. I wish I could have said good-by to my brother Michael." I sat quietly and prepared for the impact as my car would surely be pushed over the side of the cliff and burst into flames.

Instead, a kind of peace surrounded me. It felt like I was inside a bubble. Time slowed down. The squeal of tires, the burning rubber, the clouds of dust obscuring the truck occurred in slow motion. When everything stopped and became eerily quiet, the pickup truck that had been spinning towards me had miraculously stopped 10 feet from my car.

My first instinct was to get as far away as possible, so I floored the gas pedal and sped past the two SUVs. I drove about a mile away and turned off the side of the road. The driver of the sedan behind me slowed down to look at me, then sped past. I was shaking like a leaf.

I had been driving that highway for four years and had never come close to being in an accident.

In retrospect, what had I been thinking on my way home from work that day? I had begun to question my decision to leave a secure but frustrating career.

The Universe responded in no uncertain terms.

After my near-death experience, I did not need any further confirmation.

A week later I began a new journey into an uncertain future.

There was no turning back.

Chapter Three

THE CALM BEFORE THE STORM

IT ALL BEGAN ONE DAY DURING THE first weekend in January, 2014.

I was driving home from church. It was an unusually warm California day, so I drove to a shady parking spot by the Laguna Niguel public library, one of the few libraries open seven days a week. I wanted to relax, enjoy the sounds of nature, and maybe take a quick nap. It was a beautiful sunny afternoon with just a hint of a breeze, so I rolled down the windows to take in a few minutes of respite before returning home.

I drifted off to sleep and upon awakening, I observed a late model foreign car parked nearby in the shade. I saw a parrot and two dogs inside the car. Curiosity compelled me to take a closer look. I did not see anyone inside the car, but I noticed that the car was full of clothing, towels, and personal items. I also spotted a bowl of water close to the driver's side of the car.

A young woman with long brown hair approached me. She had been inside the library. She introduced herself to me and confirmed what I suspected: she was homeless and living out of her car with her animals. She told me enough of her story to have waved a number of red flags in my face. This was a woman who saw herself as a victim and wanted to be rescued.

If only I knew then what I learned later on.

I wanted to lend a hand, but I had limited resources. I had three young cats at home so inviting her and her pets to stay in my house was out of the question. I gave her $50, my text number, and a temporary arrangement for her to shower at the community pool house bathroom in my neighborhood. I promised her I would reach out to people in my church to see if anyone could provide any help with housing or work.

Talk about "signs and wonders." I was looking into my own future and didn't even know it. In four months I would lose my own home, and this woman was a mirror of things to come.

Thus began my descent into loss and homelessness.

Chapter Four

THE PERFECT STORM COMETH

BEFORE WE GO ANY FURTHER, I WANT to clarify a few things.

Reflecting on my past, I made choices most responsible adults would consider questionable. Yes, I was in what some people would call "dire straits." I lived beyond my means. I owed back taxes to the Fed and State. To hold on to my job, I had to spend $1,000 each month on repairs for my car, which had over 200,000 miles on it. I would borrow money to pay for the car repairs and pay the loan back as soon as I received my salary check at the beginning of each month. This put me deeper and deeper into debt.

I also commuted 100 miles each day to go to work and back. I would wake up at 3:45 a.m., leave the house by 6 a.m., and reach school by 7:15 a.m. Sometimes I would not arrive home until after 6 p.m. Each day was a tough day, leaving me exhausted and worn down.

What I want to say is that knowing what I do now, I could have done things differently, made other choices, and certainly more practical decisions.

Now, however, I would not change anything I did or do anything differently.

In 1993, internationally renowned author Maya Angelou (1928-2014) penned a memoir entitled, *Wouldn't Take Nothing for My Journey Now.* Her story describes her experiences as a young black girl in Stamps, Arkansas and her struggles with disappointments, injustice, betrayals, and the racial segregation of the Jim Crow era. As a young woman, she flourished as a singer and dancer, making a professional reputation for herself in both the states and Europe. Through her work as an author, poet, scholar, and civil rights activist, she transformed into a wise and respected Elder, serving as a role model and mentor to countless admirers. Angelou attributed her success to the entirety of her life experiences, embracing the value of both the positive and negative ones.

Keeping It Real

Was my loss—the home, the job, the money, and security—painful? You bet. I felt utterly alone. There were times I cried myself to sleep at night. There were times I thought about driving over a cliff and ending my misery. I hated the mental anguish, the uncertainty and feeling of helplessness. I despised the feeling that everything I had lived and worked for had come to nothing.

That was my grief speaking. The loathing I felt for myself, and my situation blinded me most days and nights.

One thing I knew was that I could not STAY in self-pity. That would get me nowhere REAL fast. It is very toxic, and who wants to be around THAT?

I was very lucky to have friends and a spiritual community who helped me through. Some gave me money. Others gave me a couch to sleep on. Others gave me encouragement and upliftment. There were strangers—people I did not even know—who helped me. The ones that I would have normally expected to help were silent or critical.

Nothing In Life Is A Mistake

Life is a classroom. We learn by doing. There are many decisions to choose from. There is a saying from the *Tao* that a person can choose from many different paths, but they ultimately all arrive at the same destiny.

Destiny is a funny thing. We like to think we have free will and freedom to choose. But I have come to believe that some of us are "marked." Not punished or rewarded, but something we individually agreed to experience before we come into this life. No one would willingly volunteer to experience the tragic, untimely death of a child unless there was some higher purpose involved.

I know that sounds other-worldly, but it is the only reasonable explanation I can come up with for why horrific things happen to people. There is so much we do not know or understand.

I used to spend a lot of time wondering "Why?" I may never know the exact answer, but I do not need to know "why" to overcome my circumstances. I just need to take one day at a time and put one foot in front of the other.

Eventually, I reach my destination.

Chapter Five

DON'T BLOCK THE BLESSINGS!

"Rabbi, Is there a blessing for sewing machines?"
"There is a blessing for everything."
from Fiddler on the Roof, (1971)

LIVING IN GRATITUDE IS THE MOST important lesson I learned from this experience. It saved me from falling through the cracks and helped me get a new start in life.

Living in gratitude comes in many forms. Bloom where you are planted. Be content in all things. Look for the blessings. Find the pony in the pile of manure. When life gives you lemons, make lemonade.

Living a life of gratitude is a mindset that involves a different way of perception and behaving. First, I learned to appreciate the value in all things and find the blessings—even in a pile of manure. I began to acknowledge things that I took for granted. Can I breathe? Can I see? Can I hear? Can I walk and dress unassisted? These are activities that thousands of people worldwide struggle with daily. If you aren't one of them, it's time to count your blessings and feel grateful!

Living in gratitude when done daily whether in prayer, affirmation or journaling, retrains the brain and redirects our focus. If we think our circumstances are bad, there is always someone else who is worse off. That immediately changes our mindset.

The Internet and YouTube are full of true stories about people who have overcome debilitating physical trauma, such as third-degree burns over 90% of their body that have left them looking like a pile of melted rubber; or the woman who was attacked and horribly disfigured by her friend's pet chimpanzee; or the young man in Indonesia whose body is afflicted by a tree-growing disease.

From Surviving to Thriving

As human beings, we are a resilient lot and driven to overcome our challenges by finding ways to cope. We decide to find something of value to live for, be it a loved one, family, or ourselves. Thriving requires us to let go of what we've lost and refrain from self-pity. Realizing that someone, somewhere, is always worse off is a good starting point.

Over time, our self-image and the world we experience begin to evolve. As a result, our outer circumstances become different.

But don't expect miracles to happen overnight. It's our job to find things to appreciate and to recognize the blessings in adversity. I begin my day by saying "Thank you for my life and thank you for my body" while I am still in bed in the morning. I make a list of five things I am grateful for and write them down. In the evening, I write five other things I am grateful for. For example, I'm thankful to be alive. I appreciate the comfortable bed I sleep in. I love my house. I'm thankful to have a car to drive. I cherish my family and friends. I'm so lucky I have a job. I'm grateful for the money in my wallet. I love having clean hot water from the shower. I'm so happy that all my organs are whole, healthy and complete.

You get the idea.

No matter what our current circumstances are or how crummy, we can ALWAYS find something to be grateful for. ALWAYS!

One thing I have always admired about the Jewish religion is its open acknowledgement of grace in every moment.

If you are going through a bad experience, or if you are one of the "walking wounded" in the aftermath of a divorce or bankruptcy, it is important to honor your feelings. Don't forget to find the blessing. Find the good, no matter how small. It will take away some of the sting and start you on the way to healing.

There comes a time when the healing process wants to take over and begin the journey back to wholeness--

if you allow it. To assist in the process, identify a blessing in your life and hold it up in front of your face to acknowledge it. Do this every day, and when you can count more blessings than negatives, Congratulations! You are well on your way to wholeness!

Chapter Six

COPING WITH OTHER PEOPLES' RESISTANCE

ONE OF THE MOST PERPLEXING ISSUES I encountered during my journey was the fear that people have around helping others.

I remember television sitcoms about the friend or relative who comes to visit for a brief time. Six months later, this same person is lounging around in a night-gown or underwear on the living room couch and being a mooch. A more recent real-life story involved the nanny who refused to leave the house of her employers after she was fired from her position. A practitioner at my church even told me she was afraid she would "get stuck" with me if I stayed in her 3-bedroom home which she lived in by herself.

During my journey, I was unprepared to deal with being seen as a pariah. It was as though my circumstances could somehow be contagious to them.

In my naivete, I discovered how quickly fear and panic can set in. I eventually came to understand why someone would not welcome a familiar acquaintance into their home to stay, no matter how temporary.

It's Not Personal

As soon as we think the world owes us something, our expectations can become unreasonable. One homeless woman I knew from church became bitter, resentful, and toxic because her cousin would not take her in.

A neighbor friend of mine I had known for many years lived in a two-story, four-bedroom house just up the street from me. I telephoned her to asked if I could temporarily stay with her. She abruptly ended the call and cut off all further communication. An estranged family member, whom I never reached out to, suddenly felt compelled to call and share his life philosophy of "sweeping his own side of the street" (staying out of other people's problems).

In either case, If I had allowed myself to become angry or victimized, I most likely would have scared away the kind-hearted people who DID come forward and offer help. Not taking other peoples' opinions personally--no matter how hurtful or shocking—is an invaluable practice that sets us free from expectations, disappointments, and drama.

Help that doesn't come from the people we expect doesn't make it any less valuable.

Chapter Seven

ASKING FOR HELP

I GREW UP IN A HOUSEHOLD WHERE asking for help was an admission of failure. Children were to be seen and not heard, and if I had a problem, my parents expected me to find a solution on my own or keep it to myself. That is how my parent's generation dealt with life. Molestation, divorce, bankruptcy, money—those issues were all taboo and hidden away as family secrets.

So, it should come as no surprise that when it came to asking other adults for help, this adult did not even consider such a thing. Better to suffer in silence and appear strong than to let anyone know I screwed up.

One of the most surprising experiences I have ever had was receiving help from unexpected sources that appeared out of nowhere.

While driving through a rural area of Lake Elsinore in Riverside County, I experienced an incredible miracle. My car had stopped at the intersection of a four-lane highway and "died." It was early in the morning, and other motorists drove past in a hurry to reach their destinations. I carefully considered what to do. The road was momentarily empty, so I got out of my car and walked across the highway to reach the safety of a street corner.

Or so I thought.

OMG Not Again!

Just as I reached the corner, a motorist appeared out of nowhere. He drove much too fast and clearly did not pay much attention to my stalled vehicle in his lane. He slammed on his brakes, and with tires squealing, rubber burning, smoke and loose gravel sending up clouds of dust, his skidding vehicle bore down on my defenseless car. I closed my eyes and helplessly waited for the gut-wrenching sound of the impact.

It felt like an eternity before I could gather the courage to open my eyes. Instead of hearing my poor car being crushed like an accordion, a string of expletives that would make a sailor blush exploded in the morning air. The motorist swerved in time to avoid turning the trunk of my car into some grotesque hood ornament and sped away.

What Happens Next Is A Miracle

As if on cue, people appeared out of nowhere. An out of service fire truck stopped to block traffic and enabled two good Samaritan motorists to push my car to a nearby street. A woman residing on a nearby hill quickly ran down to rescue me from the corner I mistakenly thought was safe. "I've seen so many accidents and people who got seriously injured standing in that exact same spot!" she exclaimed. She stayed with me in her bathrobe and slippers until a tow truck arrived. Not more than five minutes after I called for roadside assistance, an AAA driver appeared. He had just left his home in the immediate neighborhood.

I still look back on that day as a reminder of "angels in disguise"—suddenly there when we need them.

A Lesson In Humility

Some lessons keep repeating themselves in different ways until we finally catch on.

Despite my miraculous encounter with "divine" intervention, a similar lesson emerged not long after. Nothing prepared me for the trauma that would come from suddenly losing my home and everything I had worked for materially for over 50 years.

April, 2014. My rent was paid through the month, but I was in such a state of shock and denial that I felt numb and paralyzed. I tried to cope with the overwhelm of needing to vacate the house with all my belongings by the end of the month. I tried to do it all by myself, and nothing got done.

And I had no place to go.

Goddesses To The Rescue!

I finally reached out to Jenny, a friend of mine from church and a member of a select group of women known as "the Goddess Brigade." Jenny sent out the call for help to these women whom I barely knew or didn't know at all. Her cousin Cindy arranged for a local storage unit for me to use. Shana, Rachel, Sena Rose and Isabella showed up at the house to pack, discard or haul away things I knew I could not keep. Shawna and Jenny spent hours posting household items to sell on Craig's List. Isabella hauled away over 36 bags of books to the local library and purchased both my bikes. Rachel and Shawna each came on separate days to assist with packing and brought pizza for us to eat (I had no food or income).

Shana, who had bookkeeping experience, advised me to withdraw Social Security benefits since I was 62.

Ironically, if I had applied for Social Security just 4 months earlier, those payments would have possibly kept me from having to move at all.

More Help

As much as it hurt to lose my home and most of my belongings, the biggest heartbreak was relinquishing the three young kitties I had adopted and find them new homes. It was the beginning of "kitten season" and the worst time to re-home any cat. My biggest fear was that they would end up at the local city shelter. In desperation, I reached out to my friend and fellow cat lover, Dee. Between her, the Laguna Woods Cat Club and Cats Love Us Boarding, my little tribe went to an amazing boarding facility, then into foster care, and eventually found their forever homes.

Support comes in many forms. I believe God works through people, using their abilities and resources to help others.

On the other hand . . .

Chapter Eight

THE ROAD TO HELL LEADS TO A PRETTY PINK HOUSE!

"Beggars can't be choosers!"
"Don't be so picky and unappreciative!"
"What's wrong with you?!"
"Loser!"

WELL-MEANING PEOPLE CAN BE A hazard, especially in moments of trauma and shock when our self-esteem is shattered.

Unfortunately, making wise choices and optimal decisions doesn't happen when we feel vulnerable. Sometimes things work out. At other times, friends and relatives may not always be as helpful as they believe.

At the beginning of my journey, I failed to properly research living arrangements and shelter in advance.

Whether from denial or naivety, I didn't think I deserved anything better. I was so desperate that I ended up settling for anything, regardless of how shameful. On one occasion, some friends tried to organize a rental arrangement for me with a woman who had a four-year prison record, no car, and no income other than state disability payments.

And guess who was going to be on the hook legally for the lease agreement?

I recognized the pitfalls right away and nixed the idea.

In a different situation, I rented a room from a dental technician who resided in a house owned by her ex-husband in another state. A week after she accepted my check for the first month's rent, the woman called and asked me if I would mind seven Korean foreign exchange students occupying another part of the house. I said I don't mind so long as they use your bathroom and not the one I'm paying to use for myself.

Right before my move-in day, I received a voicemail from the woman. The woman's ex-husband advised her that she had the right to change her mind about me moving in, since we didn't sign a rental agreement. She returned my rental check by leaving it in pieces under the front door mat.

A year later, a mutual acquaintance told me the woman lost her job and subsequently the house.

Welcome To The Pretty Pink (Flop) House

The same friends who tried to match me up with the ex-convict told me about a woman who owned a pretty pink house in "lovely" Monterey Park, a smoggy suburb of east Los Angeles. I never spoke directly to this woman. All the communication came through one of the two friends. Any email contact I did receive from the owner was ambiguous and evasive.

There was a spare bed I could sleep on, and I could stay there rent-free. I had been staying in an upstairs room in another friend's house, but her adult son had just graduated from college and wanted to return to his mother's house to live. I had no choice but to take a leap of faith, move out, and hope that this new opportunity would be successful.

Down The Rabbit Hole

I had never been to Monterey Park in my entire adult life. Driving there and hoping for the best, I was in for a rude awakening.

June, a summer month, brings together heat, smog, and car fumes to produce greasy black particles in the air. To add to my discomfort, every store sign I saw was either in Asian, Spanish, or Arabic. No English anywhere.

How the hell was I supposed to find a job in this community?

Once I found the house, it was unmistakably pink. Pepto Bismol pink. Five parked cars were crowded together in the driveway. The front yard was dirt, and the sides of the house were overgrown with weeds. There were no curtains on the windows. Because of the crowded street parking, I had to leave my car a block away. I crossed my fingers that my car would still be there the next day. My intuition told me to conceal my belongings and leave them inside the car. Holding my nose from the smog and black particles in the air, I walked to the house with only my purse.

When I arrived at the front porch, the door was wide open. I rang the doorbell several times until a young man yelling on his cell phone came to the door. I told him my name and said the owner's son was expecting me. The young man went into the hallway and knocked on a door.

Shock And Awe

I stepped inside to wait and sat on the only chair in the living area. I surveyed the living space and felt my stomach churning. There were no curtains—anywhere. There were wall-to-wall clothes and laundry, cardboard boxes, assorted sports equipment, and no other furniture. The floor of the bathroom by the front entryway looked gross and filthy from months of neglect. The young man with the cell phone had his blanket and sleeping bag spread out all over the living room floor.

Finally, a young man emerged from the hallway. He appeared to be in a stupor. He asked me what I wanted. I told him my name and said that his mother assured me he would be expecting me, and I had her permission to live in the house.

Whatever substance he was on, he could not have cared less who I was or why I was there. Without a word, he quietly walked past me and made his way to the bathroom, where he urinated with the door wide open. When he was done, he passed me to return to his room and said, "Talk to Cookie."

Not Alice In Wonderland

By now it was past 2 p.m. I honestly did not know what to do. Whether I was in a state of shock or just physically numb, I could not even think clearly. The young man with the cell phone was quite chatty and told me he was expecting an inheritance and had been living in a van when he heard about the "pink house." He had been there a month already. I asked him where my room might be, and he pointed to a corner by the kitchen where there was a child's mattress on the floor. "That's where the owner sleeps when she stays over. Usually, though, she lives with her daughter."

I circled the living room to avoid stepping on the young man's blanket and sleeping bag. I reached the child-sized mattress on the floor and saw that it was surrounded by boxes, paper grocery bags and piles of clothes. It was right underneath a large window with no curtains. And it was next to the young man's sleeping bag.

Add "No Privacy" to the list of amenities.

The young man warned me NOT to leave any valuables or belongings in sight anywhere. Things had a way of disappearing, especially since Cookie was the only person who had a job.

Enter "Cookie"

Cookie was my age, streetwise and down to earth. She had the only decent bedroom in the house, and the only clean bathroom by her room that was for her exclusive use. She acted as House Manager for the owner. Besides herself, the other residents included the owner's two adult sons, one of whom lived in the garage with a girlfriend, a middle-aged woman who shuffled into the kitchen in her nightgown and talked as if she was on drugs, and the newest resident, the "trust baby." When Cookie first moved in five years earlier, the house had mold, and Cookie ended up in the hospital. She threatened to notify the Health Department, but she and the owner came to some sort of understanding, which included removing the mold. Cookie did not own a car but took a bus to her job in West Los Angeles.

She and I talked for two hours. I filled her in on my circumstances. Being unfamiliar with the area, I had to find a job and start earning money. She was very direct with me, but in a friendly way. No, there was no bedroom waiting for me. Yes, the child's mattress on the floor was the only sleeping accommodation available. Yes, the community bathroom that looked like a raw sewage plant was the only bathroom facility available. Yes, I could use the refrigerator but at my own risk. The only food that was not "poached" (stolen) was moldy. Yes, it was a very good idea to not have anything of value in the house.

And no, it was not a good idea for me to stay there.

That is all I needed to hear.

I thanked her for her time, got into my car with a sigh of relief and headed into rush-hour traffic for the ride back to Orange County. Even if I had to spend the night in my car, I was certain I would sleep better than if I had stayed overnight in the pink house.

On a hunch, I contacted the manager of the church I belonged to and asked if I could spend the night on the couch in one of the upstairs rooms. She checked with the minister, who graciously agreed, and that is where I stayed, off and on, for the next several months.

My Come-To-Jesus Moment

That day was a turning point for me. It was a harsh wake-up call, but I gained two valuable lessons:

"Look before you leap." I did not do MY due diligence and check out the accommodations before I arrived to move in.

The second lesson was much deeper and insightful. Human behavior has a remarkable capacity to adapt to adverse circumstances. For the people who lived in the "pink house," drugs, theft and squalor had become their "normal." They lived under those conditions for so long that they lost their ability to realize anything different.

And unless I wanted to become just like them, I had to find another way.

As my younger brother once said so delicately, "When people live in their own filth long enough, they don't notice how bad it smells."

I have heard experts warn that the longer a person is homeless, the more likely that person is to remain homeless. They have become conditioned to their new "normal."

That day, as shocking as it was, turned out to be a blessing in disguise. The flophouse experience brought me as close to rock-bottom as I have ever been, then and now.

It took something like this to scream, "THIS IS NOT YOU!"

And I finally heard.

"In my pain, there inside my weakness,
Is the seed of something . . . Greater . . . in me
And the shame of not choosing higher
All the disappointing moments
Fade into God.
No mistakes have been made in God
All the ways that we seem to fail
In God All fade . . .
But the stars shining are to remind us
The Seed will need the darkness to change into new light.
And no mistakes have been made in God."

Excerpt from "All Fades Into God," composed by Rickie Byars and Michael Beckwith and reprinted here with kind permission from Eternal Dance Music, BMI ©2000.

Chapter Nine

BE CAREFUL WHAT YOU WISH FOR

IN A RUSH TO ESCAPE FROM THE LITTLE house of horrors, I anxiously called the office manager of the church I attended in Orange County to ask for a place to stay overnight. Meanwhile, the well-intentioned friend who initially directed me to the "pretty pink house" was now calling to advise me to drive to a different location for housing 25 miles away.

I was learning fast, and this time I had the presence of mind to ask some questions. No, she wasn't sure about the availability. No, she hadn't been in touch with the current residents. Her request was for me to simply drive over, appear at a stranger's doorstep, and assume they would take me in.

I had had enough rabbit holes and disappointments for one day, and I adamantly refused to go on another wild goose chase. I was returning to Mission Viejo. I have no recollection of the drive back, but I do remember how I cried in relief when I pulled into the church parking lot and opened the front door. The minister contacted me, gave me permission to stay overnight and scheduled a meeting for the following day.

That night I slept on a massage table that I put up against a wall in the nursery room. It wasn't much, but I was so very grateful to feel I was among friends. Following our meeting the next day, the minister graciously agreed to let me sleep in one of the empty rooms upstairs until I could determine my next steps. She probably believed this would last for a week or even a month.

Welcome To The "Dew Drop Inn"

Except for two failed attempts to rent a room in someone's home, I did not move out for good for nearly a year. I kept my sleeping arrangement quiet and only a few other people knew. I was always there to open the main office in the morning and close up after the conclusion of classes or other events. I saw and heard a lot. It was like being a fly on the wall. If those walls ever spoke!

I took my morning shower at the local YMCA right around the corner, but I was especially grateful for access to a private restroom at night after church was closed. The only time I ever had to hustle was on a Sunday morning. I had to fold up the massage table, clear all my personal items and haul everything downstairs to put in my car. I made sure to wash and dress in the church restroom before 6 a.m. as the first minister would arrive to set up the coffeepot for church services.

Over the months I learned to make myself useful and help where I could. I don't think either minister knew how many people would come and go after hours. Occasionally, band members would stay overnight after other performances rather than drive to their homes in other counties. There were times an individual needed somewhere to sleep because of transportation difficulties. They would arrange some chairs in the main sanctuary and create a makeshift bed. Other people might drop in after office hours to prepare for some future event. The cleaning people were as surprised as I was when they entered my room at 4 a.m. and found me asleep. Then there were the class instructors who left their belongings behind and had to retrieve them—at 1 a.m.

There was a security code on the front door, but it seemed like everybody knew the code. We had so many volunteers on so many committees that it was easy for anyone to enter the building at any time.

And they did!

One of the ministers wryly referred to the situation as, "the do drop in."

I was never afraid to be alone. In fact, I welcomed the peace and quiet. The only unnerving incident was the morning the fire alarm went off in the entire building. The business tenant at the opposite end of the property accidentally set off the fire alarm—and ceiling sprinklers—in their offices. I was in the restroom wearing only pajamas and brushing my teeth when the fire department truck arrived at church with sirens blaring and lights flashing. A firefighter pounded on the door to ask where the water main was. I was the wrong person to ask! Fortunately, he found it and cut the alarm as well. I called the ministers at home to let them know disaster had been averted!

When I finally did locate other housing and moved out, I left a card for the ministers quoting one of my favorite Bible verses from Psalm 27:

"One thing have I asked of the Lord: to dwell in the house of the Lord all the days of my life, to gaze upon the beauty of the Lord and to seek Him in His temple."

Who knew there would come such a day!

Chapter Ten

MY HEALING JOURNEY BEGINS

"There is a road, a journey we must take
That starts from within
And is just a thought away.
I have got a song
That the flowers gave to me
And it helps me to be strong,
And it helps me to be free."

Excerpt from "Walking with God," composed by Rickie Byars & Michael Beckwith and reprinted here with kind permission from Eternal Dance Music, BMI ©2000

IN TRUTH, THE HEALING PROCESS HAD already begun. I just didn't know it.

Sunday, May 11, 2014 was Mother's Day. It had been barely a week since I had left behind my dream home with only my clothes and a few personal items in my car.

At the very last moment, I received a temporary but welcome invitation to spend a week or two in someone's guest room. A member of the Goddess Brigade had recently been hired as a personal assistant to a well-known Hollywood socialite. As I drove up the steep, winding road to an exquisite three-story home in the West Hollywood hills, I caught sight of the breathtaking panoramic view overlooking Los Angeles. There was a spare room with a daybed waiting for me. I had high hopes of getting a job or finding work in a media company. After all, this was Hollywood, the city of dreams and aspirations.

Our socialite-hostess was kind enough to share her food and even prepared dinner for us. The third story was also home to a chef and his cat, "Blacky." Blacky occasionally came down the spiral staircase to check on any new disturbances. Animals have always been present in my life, so I welcomed the chance to connect with a new cat. I never met Blacky's owner, but the personal assistant cautioned me about Blacky's mean temperament and advised me to avoid him. I quickly discovered this was not true. Blacky was lonely and hungry for attention. Our friendship developed rapidly, and Blacky would actively look for me and stay by my side whenever I was inside the house.

After a few weeks, the job search yielded no results, and my respite in West Hollywood ended. I loaded up my car and went back to Orange County, where I had another invitation to stay in a friend's spare room.

I left so abruptly that I never got to say goodbye to Blacky and explain why I had to leave. (Yes, I am an animal empath and can "talk to the animals"). The young woman who originally invited me said Blacky would come every day to the guestroom where I stayed and wait for me. Eventually, he stopped coming and remained with his owner upstairs.

The Sirens Beckon!

But on this Mother's Day, I found myself alone in this big empty house. Everyone else had some place to go or someone to visit. I was still reeling from the last two months and yearned for solace and comfort.

I walked outside to the backyard patio and took in the spectacular view of the city. It was a beautiful sunny morning with a haze hanging above the horizon. The tranquil return of nostalgic old songs interrupted my reverie. In my imagination, I began to recall the lyrics of melodies from happier times in the past. Music has always been an important part of my life. It inspires, uplifts and renews the weariest of souls!

It came as little surprise when I found my attention drawn to a familiar southwest location from where I stood. The Agape International Church in nearby Culver City was a short distance from the Hollywood Hills, and I was thrilled by the prospect of being "with the Mother" on this day. As I was leaving, Blacky the cat found me. I told him I would return in a few hours.

Welcome To Agape!

This was not my first visit to Agape. Even though I was a member of another church, the mythos and stories surrounding Rev. Dr. Michael Beckwith and his "beloved community" compelled more than mere curiosity.

I cannot recall the date of my first visit, but I never forgot the love and sense of well-being that filled the 3,000-seat auditorium. People traveled from all over to attend one or more of the three services on Sunday morning. Rev. Beckwith achieved what Dr. Martin Luther King had envisioned: a diverse community brought together in unity and the desire to serve.

While Rev. Michael may have been the intellectual leader, his wife Rickie was the "heart" of Agape. A gifted singer, songwriter, and musician in her own right, she became its first Musical Director. Her contagious energy and joyous spirit grew the Agape International Choir to as many as 200 members. Singing, chanting, and dancing to the spirited songs at the start of each service made sitting still impossible!

Hearing the music now again, the lyrics spoke to me in a way that other songs did not. Rickie's voice carried a vibration of solace and ancient healing. Ever since losing my home and familiar routine, I had been overwhelmed with feelings of hopelessness, confusion, and isolation.

But on this day, the loving energy of everyone around pulled me out of my despair. As an empath, I am very sensitive to places, and I immediately felt a change come over me. The music, choir, band, Miss Rickie's singing, and Rev. Michael's inspiring message turned my emptiness into something positive to embrace. The lyrics became words to live by, and some felt as if they were written just for me.

After that day, and even after I moved back to Orange County, I attended all three Sunday services whenever I could afford the gas it took to drive to Agape and back. I could not get enough. Something deep inside resonated with the melodies, the lyrics, and the "angelic" voices of the choir.

There were many, many unforgettable events I experienced during my time at Agape One of the most mesmerizing, exquisite songs I have ever heard performed was the Gayatri Mantra, an ancient Hindu chant that is believed to purify and balance the mind and spirit. Accompanied by the Agape International Choir, soloist Reirani Taurima elevated the sacred essence of Sanskrit to a timeless realm while holding her sleeping infant to her breast. It is a memory that still haunts me and gives me goosebumps even after all these years!

Thus began a new journey to heal my heart and chaotic life. Despite facing many hurdles and challenges, I continued to grow stronger and conquer my challenges.

As for Agape, it saddened me to learn that the Beckwiths split up in 2018. I knew it would divide the church, but somehow "the beloved community" would prevail. Rev. Michael forged ahead with a smaller ministry in a more manageable location. Rickie Byars re-discovered the freedom of shining her own light and being recognized for the musical channel that she is.

They are the embodiment of resilience.

Resilience is about finding the strength to bounce back. Finding the good in adversity is about recognizing the love that is inherent in each person and each endeavor. I am forever grateful for the healing I received that continues to sustain me in good times and bad.

Chapter Eleven

YOUR A__ IS MINE, SAYETH THE LORD

OR, SOME OF THE REASONS I BELIEVE "stuff" happens.

I offer this up for those who have wondered, as I have, why me?

You are cruising along, thinking life is good, all is well, and then you hit a brick wall.

WHAM!

You have been unexpectedly fired or released from your job. The love of your life hands you the divorce papers, or worse, you find the love of your life in bed with someone else. You go in for a routine physical and receive news that you only have months to live. Your business partner has cleaned out your business account and has left the country. Your teenage son or daughter commits suicide.

On a global level, every year there are catastrophic fires, storms, earthquakes, tsunamis, and floods that leave thousands displaced or homeless.

Loss of any kind is a normal part of living. Traumatic loss, like the ones described above, really puts us to the screws. The benefit is we find out what kind of person we are and what we are really made of.

And if we work it right, we can transform that awareness into a new foundation.

One thing is certain: we are meant to thrive.

Spoiler Alert: We Are Not In (Complete) Control

Many years after the 10-year ordeal she described in her book, *Peace from Broken Pieces*, Life Coach and International Best-Selling author Iyanla Van Zant was interviewed on radio by Rev. Dr. Michael Beckwith. Van Zant had experienced every kind of loss imaginable: her husband left her for her best friend. She owed thousands of dollars in back taxes to the IRS. She lost her dream home. Her publisher of 20 years terminated her contract. Her TV show got canceled. Her personal and business relationship with early benefactor Oprah Winfrey was in shreds.

If there was anyone who had an excuse to stay in bed rather than face the day, it was her.

Van Zant survived all of that, but when her beloved 33-year-old daughter Gemmia succumbed to a rare form of cancer, she was so overwhelmed by grief that she spent the next six months in bed in a fetal position.

During the interview, Van Zant revealed that the number one surprise she learned from her 10-year experience was the lack of control she had over her life. It did not matter how many self-improvement books she read or authored, or affirmations she faithfully recited; seminars and workshops she attended, or tapes and CDs she listened to. Contrary to the popular message of the New Age culture of which she was a part, Van Zant did NOT have complete control over her life's destiny, including any "detours" that might come along.

Instead, Spirit whispered in her ear: "Oh, Sister, have we got a lesson for You!"

No Matter How Far We Stray

So, when tragedy, upheaval, chaos, or traumatic loss disrupts our lives, is it random or some sort of divine intervention?

I believe there is a general blueprint our soul selects before each incarnation. While there may be some random events, the lessons all point in the same direction.

Others will argue that nothing happens by coincidence or accident. Everything in our lives is pre-ordained, from the selection of our parents to our heritage, family, neighbors, friends, work, or career. Marriage partners, where we live and what we do are chosen before birth for the purpose of our spiritual growth.

I believe the truth lies somewhere in the middle. The movie *Forest Gump* beautifully depicts the delicate lilting balance between the conscious choices we make and seemingly random events. However, our destination is the same. We ultimately end up where we are supposed to be. Much like the white feather floating in the air at the beginning of Gump's story, life weaves and bobs but eventually comes full circle and finds its way back to its intended path.

I believe our lives follow a similar direction. We have freedom of choice, but when we deviate too far from our destiny, Spirit brings us back, sometimes leading us gently by the ear, and sometimes kicking and screaming.

Where Is The Love?

Behind every so-called calamity that happens, there is at least one spiritual reason or lesson underneath. We are given warnings, softly at first, but if ignored, a hard kick in the butt is next. Be it divorce, death of a spouse, a health scare, loss of a job or a home. Little whispers come at first, growing louder, until there is a scream. The reality we once knew no longer exists. The familiar way of doing things no longer applies. This is where the rubber meets the road, and we either adapt to the changes or die holding onto what was.

The Moment Of Truth

When we realize in our bones that the reins of control are no longer in the hands of our ego but in the grasp of something much bigger than ourselves, we have two options. We can fight it with our ego intact and flounder around trying to make sense of it. Or we can cooperate, relax, and allow ourselves to be shown and guided by this greater force.

Trusting the unseen and surrendering to it is a spiritual struggle against our ego's need for control and survival. It is a difficult process because it is contrary to everything we have been taught and conditioned to believe. Embracing this way of living is like choosing between a train or a sailboat.

Some of us are fortunate enough to emerge from a traumatic loss unscathed; and in our newly found wisdom, we decide we never want to return to our self-centered, chaotic existence.

But there are those who have been rewarded for their scars and wounds with that rarest of all insight: We live in a benign universe that loves us so much that it guides us through one painful experience after another to a more loving, conscious, purpose-filled life.

It is always with us.

It never leaves or abandons us.

In fact, it IS us.

EPILOGUE

THERE WAS A TIME WHEN I LONGED FOR my old life. I longed for my dream home in Laguna Niguel, my mornings spent swimming in the pool or going to the gym. I delighted in playing with my three kitties and enjoying their playful antics. I leisurely worked on my writing projects in the afternoon and early evening.

What I don't miss is living above my means and constantly being behind on my rent or bills. I don't miss worrying about making car payments or maintaining a car with 200,000 miles or the $1,000 a month repair bills to keep it running. My finances are simple, and I live frugally with an occasional splurge now and then. I am at peace with my circumstances, even though I don't know what tomorrow brings or what the future holds. I have learned to let go of the need to control and be more like the feather in the wind or the sailboat following the open current.

Instead of drifting aimlessly, however, there is a pathway I am guided to follow. I have learned to look for clues and signs and think symbolically. I have learned to trust my intuition and expect that all my real needs are met.

Buckminster Fuller once observed that the Universe provides for even the smallest sparrow. The Bible says the same thing: "Consider the lilies of the field, how they grow. They toil not, neither do they spin" (Matthew 6:28).

There is a loving, compassionate care about all living things in a benevolent universe. That is not to say that there aren't challenges and difficulties, as we can tell from this book. For every problem, a solution arrived. It may not have come packaged the way I expected—or the way my ego wanted—but I learned to surrender and accept what was offered, even if I had to reject it later on.

I realize that all the mishaps, mistakes, detours, and course corrections were leading me to my right path all along. The same presence that appears as a kindly stranger at the right moment. The delay that causes us to miss a train stop that has an accident on the very route we missed. The perfect "soulmate" who stood us up, and many years later we discover how closely we dodged a bullet and avoided a disastrous relationship.

When we have faith and trust in a benevolent universe that has our back, we can relax our grasp and surrender to that path of being in the flow and being in alignment with our destiny.

It's at that point that we finally realize that life, especially the challenges and jagged edges, is always all about the love.

"I'm ready to listen now
I've heard Your voice before.
Your way has been calling me
Now I'm ready to be so much more.
I'm ready to listen now,
I'm ready to listen."

Excerpt from "I'm Ready to Listen," composed by Rickie Byars and Michael Beckwith and reprinted here with kind permission from Eternal Dance Music, BMI ©2000.

THE END

A MESSAGE FROM THE AUTHOR:

Thank you for investing your valuable time in reading my book.

If you have received any positive value from this reading experience, would you be willing to do me and future readers a HUGE favor by providing honest feedback on Amazon.com?

As a new publisher I would truly appreciate knowing what you liked about the book. What did you find helpful or useful?

Your feedback needn't be extensive. Short and to the point works best.

Thank You in advance,

Cheryl Cuttineau
Happy At Home Publishing

APPENDIX A: TOSHA SILVER

Aligning With The Divine

So, how do we find this ability to let go and allow life to direct our path?

I would like to refer liberally to the contemporary work of Tosha Silver, a San Francisco mystic, author of four books, a teacher of spiritual pragmatism, and facilitator of a popular weekly podcast. Her second book, *Change Me Prayers*, was my lifeline and bible during the early years of my journey. She introduced me to the concept of surrendering desires and wants to what she calls the Divine Beloved. We can call it God, the Universe, Aunt Bee, or Jesus. The idea is to release and let go of ego demands that keep us stuck and unhappy.

Buddhism says that all unhappiness is caused by our attachments. They often take the form of addictions to shopping, cars, clothes, sex, food, houses, the perfect mate, the latest gadgets, even books and religion or spirituality. In short, anything we find ourselves dependent on emotionally, physically, or mentally. The principal theme of *Change Me Prayer*s is to change oneself instead of seeking to change outer conditions and other people. Happiness is an inside job.

Social Conditioning

In her fourth book, *It's Not Your Money*, Tosha pulls back the curtain on how our culture conditions us to grasp and control everything and everyone around us. How many people in our culture are addicted to being politically correct and morally superior to those who don't agree with our political or religious beliefs? Freedom of speech and expression of thought are all but banned from our university campuses. Today, Angela Davis would be chased off the UCLA campus if she had been on the "wrong" (read "different") side of someone else's fence.

While her fourth book is about changing one's relationship and attitude towards money and abundance, there is a testimonial on the last page by one of Tosha's students that beautifully sums up the whole of Tosha's work:

"I have only one huge regret—that I never gave my life to something beyond my daily desires. I had two great children and so many chances to be creative. But every step of the way, I only did what I thought would make *me* happy. I never once asked God, How can I serve *You?* I mean, really, how can I serve *You*?

Who knows what might have happened if I had?"

(p. 163)

For more information about Tosha and her classes, please visit toshasilver.com.

APPENDIX B: TWO INSPIRING STORIES

When we feel isolated, it becomes quite easy to feel sorry for ourselves. In the seven years I was homeless, I often felt alone in my situation.

To counter this tendency, I connected with others through social media. It was here that I learned I was not alone. There were hundreds, perhaps thousands, of people who had been downsized from their longtime careers and were left trying to re-enter a younger market or reinvent themselves. Even though it was 2014, long-term unemployment, age discrimination, loss of support, depression, trauma and grief were in full force following the fallout from the 2008 economic wrecking ball.

The Will To Overcome

Two life stories stand out in my recollection. The first one proves that there is always someone somewhere who is worse off. We cannot afford the luxury of self-pity. In a post on Facebook, a young woman chronicled her 10 years of struggle and hardship. She and her boyfriend were living in her parents' basement and being supported by them. Her car was old and broke down frequently in the cold and snow. It had no heater and was missing windows. The woman had a job, but transportation issues frequently interfered with her ability to keep her job.

She and her boyfriend finally found an abandoned school building for rent. There was no electricity nor running water inside, and they would have to rent an outside porta-potty. Winter was extremely challenging, as you can imagine, but they were young and were elated to be finally on their own. Showering outside in the snow with an outside hose didn't seem so bad, so long as they had each other.

So they managed to thrive. This same woman reported 10 years later that she is a stay-at-home mom with two young children, and her former boyfriend-now-husband had a steady job with a good enough income to support a growing family. They were living comfortably in a leased condo with an option to buy. Their future looked full of promise.

Her advice? "Never, ever give up."

Gratitude Trumps Disaster

In 2015, California wildfires ravaged thousands of neighborhoods, leaving many to spend their Christmas holidays at the makeshift Red Cross shelters. A television reporter was interviewing an older couple whose home in the high desert area had burned to the ground. They were sitting inside their subcompact car with their small dog and all the clothes they could fit in the backseat and trunk. There was no sob story, no woe is me attitude. This couple was smiling. They were joking with the reporter. Their little dog was in the backseat wagging its tail, just happy to be with his caretakers. This couple was so grateful to be alive and safe and with each other. "Everything that matters is right here," they told the reporter.

In the days and months into the future, and now years past, I have never forgotten the image of them living out of that tiny car, but grateful to be alive and unharmed. Unless they contact me, I will never know what eventually happened to them. But something tells me they turned their lives around and restored anything of true value that may have been temporarily lost.

In contemporary parlance, they did not allow their circumstances to defeat or define who they are.

# # # # #

If life has taught me anything, it is that we only fail when we stop trying and give up. This is why I believe so many men and women fall through the cracks and become lost to a life on the streets. It is too easy to succumb to a sudden traumatic loss and become lost themselves.

Unless there is someone or something that reaches deep inside and pulls them back, the path to living a normal, actualized life is extremely difficult, but not impossible. I spoke with too many homeless people who lost contact with family and friends and morphed into one of the tent cities or became panhandlers on the streets. Not everyone can be rehabilitated, but not everyone wants to remain homeless.

Encouragement Costs Nothing

If you know of someone who is struggling to deal with an emergency or challenge, offer encouragement, show you believe in them, sincerely and often. I was blessed to have such a person. I told myself, "If so-and-so believes that much in me or my ability to get out of this mess I'm in, I must be able to do it!"

Sometimes an emotional hands-up is all it takes to change the direction of someone's life.

APPENDIX C: PET LOSS

As a Certified Pet Loss & Bereavement Counselor, I would be remiss if I did not include this painful experience as one of many life losses.

I would never equate the value of the life of an animal with that of a human being. The death of a dog or cat can never equal the death of one's child; and yet, so many of us treat our animal companions as if they were our children.

The loss or death of these animals who share our lives can be just as emotionally devastating. Go to any popular dog or cat channel on Facebook on any day and you will find scores of grieving pet owners describing their broken hearts. Many others who respond describe how they are still grieving years, even decades, after their personal loss.

The unique bond that exists between pet owners/caretakers and their animal companions is so unusual that a different field of grief counseling had to be created. Pioneered by Dr. Wallace Sife (1932-2020), pet loss and bereavement counseling addresses the psychological/spiritual needs that differ from traditional grief therapy.

One of my teachers and someone I respect enormously is the world-renowned animal communicator and healer, Val Heart, aka "The Real Dr. Doolittle." She recently wrote two excellent email posts: "How to Handle the Grief of Tragic Events" and a companion post, "How to Forgive and Find True Peace with What Happened to You or Your Pet."

I hadn't even considered including pet loss in this book out of concern some people would accuse me of "trivializing" more serious forms of loss. These two blogs were the inspiration for this section being added to the book. Both posts are too lengthy to include here, but their author kindly gave me permission to summarize them here.

- Grief and pain can keep us stuck if we don't know how to release them. Journaling, EFT/Tapping, prayer, Ho'oponopono, and clinical grief therapy are some of the ways that can help us heal from lingering emotional wounds.

- As a Master Healer, Val Heart has experience with those and numerous other techniques; but the technique she hangs her hat on is an energy-based practice called the 12D Energy Detachment Exercise. It is particularly effective on empaths, highly sensitive individuals, or anyone with emotional wounds and scars.

- Betrayals, abuse, accidents, injuries, trauma, social injustices, and crimes against humanity and against animals are sources of great pain. The 12D High Energy Hygiene Practice works from the inside out. Removing triggers and wounds from the inner energy field first is essential before we can begin the forgiveness process and move forward.

For additional information or to contact Val directly, visit her website www.valheart.com.

The website is a treasure trove of information featuring her Heart Wisdom School of free ebooks, courses, programs and memberships. Highly, highly recommended, Val Heart is the "real deal."

And One More Thing

I would also like to offer my own humble website, "Nepenthes Garden," to anyone who is grieving the loss of a cherished animal companion. The inspiration for this website, including its name and color palette, came to me in a dream. No lie! Who would have thought that a flower named nepenthe was an ancient remedy for extreme grief and suffering? Not me! Even the introduction on the first page came from someone or something else!

I have since expanded it to include other features that I did research and author. A notable exception is the beautiful song by Faith Rivera on the first page. I interpret the lyrics as a tribute to a human companion left behind from a loving pet who has passed on. But it could be heard both ways. Have a listen! www.nepenthesgarden.com.

APPENDIX D: GOOD NEWS FOR THE HOMELESS?

1929 Revisited

Over the past several years, the US economy challenged us in ways that were reminiscent of the Great Depression. Images of well-dressed men standing in soup lines or sleeping on the streets in 1929 have been replaced by images of luxury automobiles waiting in line at the local drive-through food bank. In 2010, Walmart parking lots were filled after dark by homeless people living out of their cars, vans, and trailers. There were not enough emergency shelters available, and many shelters were unsafe. People in the Walmart encampments stayed together as a form of protection. Stories abounded about sex predators—men and women—and drug addicts who frequented the shelters and would knife you if he or she thought you had 50 cents in your wallet.

Meanwhile, a tsunami was developing that threatened to catch many people off guard, myself included. Housing costs began to skyrocket out of control. According to United Way, the number one cause of homelessness in Orange County, California was the intersection between a loss of income and unaffordable housing in 2015. Social workers I talked to said they were seeing unprecedented numbers of people who were unemployed and/or homeless. At one point, we had over 40,000 veterans nationwide homeless and living on the streets.

Politicians Fiddle While Rome Burns

We live in the richest, most abundant country in the world, but we allow our citizens to live in poverty and squalor. This contrast was never more evident than our government leaders from the White House borrowing billions of dollars of debt from China to give billions of dollars to fund foreign wars with absolutely no accounting of where it went and how it was used.

Meanwhile, when out-of-control fires swept through Maui, Hawaii in 2023 and burned homes and business in Lahaina to the ground, American citizens were homeless and without food or water. Our President took the time out from his busy weekend vacation at a billionaire's mansion to announce each family would receive a single, onetime $700 check to pay for housing, food and water. In that same week, the President authorized another multi-billion-dollar package to fund another foreign war, and Congress went along with it.

Clearly, Our Own Citizens Are Not A Priority

Contrast that with the response to the 2016 wildfires that raged through Sevier County, Tennessee, and left thousands homeless. Within 48 hours, Performer Dolly Parton, a native of Sevierville, used her Dollywood Foundation to establish a My People Fund and immediately issued $1,000 to every family whose home had been destroyed. These payments continued for six months. Because of public donations, the final payments were increased to $5,000 per family. A total of $12.5 million dollars went directly to victims of the wildfires.

And all it took was one person with a generous heart, the right intentions, and a love for people to take meaningful action.

Solutions: Housing First

Finland and Denmark have all but eliminated homelessness by following a policy of "Housing First." This policy recognizes the primary need for stability and traction when someone is trying to regain control over their life.

After many years of ignoring the giant elephant in the backyard, American city and county governments began to partner with United Way and other businesses to create a "Housing First" model locally. The most compelling reason for adopting this program was economic. According to United Way, it costs $55,000 a year to house a homeless person, whereas it costs nearly $450,000 annually to leave a person living on the streets. The longer a person lives on the streets, the faster his or her health deteriorates, and hospital and medical services balloon out of control. The savings to house the homeless population in California using this program is over $43 million a year, according to the United Way.

In today's world, with homelessness on the rise, providing housing alone isn't sufficient. Mental Health and rehabilitation services are a crucial factor in the success of any housing program.

Will our politicians catch on, or will they continue to play "hot potato" with the homeless issue while developers and lobbyists become rich with taxpayer funds like they do in San Diego County and other cities where homelessness continues to grow?

I'm not holding my breath.

APPENDIX E: SURVIVAL TIPS

My experience taught me the importance of being resourceful. To me, it means adjusting my resources to ensure self-protection and survival.

This Appendix/Supplement contains useful information you may need when you suddenly lose the roof over your head or don't have a car to sleep in.

Another essential lesson I learned is to avoid making important decisions during a crisis. When we are traumatized, shocked, or panicked, we don't think as clearly. While we can't predict every challenge, mentally preparing for potential upsets proves to be very useful, as I can personally attest.

I also felt it was important to update this section before publication because of the local and world disasters happening on a more frequent basis. 2023 has been declared "the year with the highest number of billion-dollar disasters on record." Fires in Hawaii, floods in Libya, earthquakes in Morocco, and cyclones and hurricanes have all caused terrible disruptions to peoples' lives worldwide.

And this does not include the wars that are currently taking place in East Europe and the Middle East as of October 2023.

To those of you who say, "It will never happen to me," I suggest you refer to the front of the book and review the names of well-known people who have been homeless. I'll bet not one of them ever planned on being homeless, even temporarily.

Think Ahead, But Don't Live in Fear

There are three sections to this Appendix. Section 1 dives into the basics of survival when we don't have a home. Section 2 explains some of my thoughts about the origins of homelessness. This book offers guidance on coping with the consequences of a traumatic loss. Whether we thrive or succumb depends on how we respond. Loss doesn't always mean homelessness, but I maintain that the seeds of homelessness are inherent in any loss.

Finally, Section 3 is for you diehards who want to read about my actual experiences, hence the section title regarding public libraries, the YMCA and Denny's.

Section 1: Survival

In my experience, the necessities I found to be important to my survival and well-being were (in no particular order):

- Shelter
- Food and Water

- Money
- Tansportation
- Clothing
- Hygiene
- A network or community of allies

By the time I was ready to leave my former dream house, I had learned to organize clothing, separate clothes that needed laundering, and store personal hygiene items inside the car trunk.

In my situation, I had a community of friends; I was an active member of a church, and I had a car with $1400 back payments owing. Thanks to a helpful friend, I became aware of my eligibility and started receiving $900 from Social Security as my only income. The kind and generous response from friends at church enabled me to rent a storage unit and buy gas and food. I also made the rounds of all the food pantries in the area. Something was better than nothing. I had lost over 25 pounds in one month alone. I put essentials into storage and disposed of everything else by selling, donating, or throwing it away.

The bank that still owned my car either did not bother to reclaim it or never found its location. All my mail went to a post office box in another town, including DMV registration, car insurance and tax returns. If I had to provide a physical address, I used a friend's address, with permission, of course. I kept up with car repairs and maintenance, insurance, and registration. That car was the difference between me and the streets.

SHELTER

This is the big one. Without it, there is no traction—no stability from which to regain one's footing and make forward progress.

Many friends allowed me to sleep on their couch, sofa, day bed, living room floor. Further along my journey, when I was working three part-time jobs, I rented furnished rooms in someone's home.

I even lived for six months in one of the spare rooms on the 2nd floor of my church. I borrowed someone's massage table as a bed and used my own blanket and pillow.

PERSONAL HYGIENE

I was fortunate to have access to a YMCA a few miles' drive from wherever I was. A warm shower and clean hair can lift anyone's mood. I had a membership, and thanks to the kindness of the director, I was eligible for a discount, and all the free coffee I could want. Any gym is fine, but ones that are open 24-7 and affordable are ideal.

CLOTHING

This might seem obvious, but what happens when the *clean* clothes run out?

One place that has never changed in my entire life is the convenience of the local laundromat. Rain or shine, good times or bad, the neighborhood laundromat has withstood the test of time.

Like anything else, not all laundromats are the same. Some are cleaner than others, have a variety of well-maintained machines, a clean restroom, an abundance of free parking, and they are in safe neighborhoods.

In my limited experience, it used to be that the only people who used a laundromat were those whose home clothes washer or dryer had broken down. They either had to wait an extended time for a repairman or could not immediately afford to repair or replace a broken appliance. Some people just plain didn't have a washer or dryer in their home or apartment. When you can get two loads done at the same time and be back home in the time it would take you to do one load of clothes, it makes more sense.

The first time I entered a laundromat when I was homeless, I noticed the kinds of people who were there. Poor people, homeless people, single dads, single moms, older adults, young adults, more than one family sharing a house. People who drove luxury cars, and people who had all their belongings in a shopping cart. Panhandlers and people who didn't have a quarter in order to use the pay-toilet. People who were adept at using the laundromat and scrupulously sanitized the clothes counters (tables) before using them. There were others who used the counters to change a baby's diaper or allow their children to run on top. It was an interesting cross-section of the community. I eventually got used to it, but it was a culture shock.

Look for the good ones in advance, be aware of what kind of neighborhood it is in and find out what forms of payment are accepted. The modern ones accept credit or debit cards but expect to have $20 in quarters available.

FOOD

I applied for food stamps at the local DPSS (Department of Social Services) and received $72 a month for 12 months. Food pantries were another resource and free. Churches and local charities offer them.

With sufficient funds, you can discover healthy dining spots such as El Pollo Loco. However, fast-food locations are not ideal when you are surviving. A steady diet of high fat, high salt and high sugar will take its toll. You don't want to starve, but your goal is to THRIVE, and you can't do that if you are sick from a poor diet.

Daily, plentiful water consumption is crucial, unless you want to end up like I did—passed out on the sidewalk and lying face down in my own blood and urine. I spent three days in the hospital recovering from dehydration and injuries to my face from passing out. Always have water on hand. If you don't want to buy bottled water, take an empty container into any fast-food restaurant and ask permission to fill it with water.

RESTROOMS

Which brings me to the next obvious necessity.

If you drink a lot of water, you will need to know where the clean public restrooms are: public libraries, family restaurants, most gas stations, large retail stores like Walmart and Target, and 24-hour gyms. I had access to clean restrooms at the storage facility I rented from, which opened early and closed at 8pm.

Another place to check out is the local hospital. I spent many a night parked in the visitor parking lot where I felt safe and used the public restroom facilities inside at night.

Section 2: Origins of Homelessness

This part is based on what I learned, observed and experienced as a member of the homeless community. I am not a professional expert with all kinds of statistics and reports. Rather, my expertise comes from over seven years of experience with homeless people and being one.

In my opinion, there is no one single cause of homelessness. That path can be triggered by events such as a devastating divorce, the tragic loss of loved ones, or the inability to rebound from a career setback. Any of us can suffer the traumatic loss of something that becomes so painful that we are overcome by depression and never recover.

I met several people like me whose out-of-control circumstances overwhelmed them and took over their lives. One such person was a former college professor whose wife divorced him. All he had left were his van and belongings. He lost his job because of budget cuts. Try as he may, he could not get rehired. He was an older gentleman, and his age may have played a part in his inability to get another teaching position. After a while, he said he just gave up. He became accustomed to living in his van and relying on government assistance. This was his new "normal."

The Reality

Not every homeless person is an alcoholic, drug addict or psychotic. Not every homeless person wants to be helped. Many people I encountered were like my professor friend: they lost hope, stopped trying, and gave up. They quickly became another statistic of someone who fell through the cracks of the social safety net. They would join the increasing population of over 650,000 homeless citizens and 39,000 veterans in the world's most prosperous country.

I wrote this book to offer Hope. There IS help if you know where to find it and are willing to swallow your pride—if only temporarily.

If you want to survive on the streets, learn to be resourceful and resilient.

If you never give up, you cannot fail.

Section 3: Thank God for Denny's, the YMCA, and Public Libraries

It used to be so much easier. Being a hobo, a gypsy, a vagabond—someone who carries their worldly possessions with them and travels from city to city. I'm talking about car-camping. I drove my car all the way around the United States when I finished college, and most of the time I did not stay in a motel or someone's home, or even a tent. I pulled off the road or parked in one of those "Rest Areas" off the highway. I slept in my car or in a sleeping bag on a cot outside. Until recently, truckers pulled into large vacant parking lots or off the road and slept inside their cab. Walmart was especially accommodating. It's a whole other culture, but no one was the worse for it.

How Times Have Changed

In many cities, sleeping in your car is now a crime, especially in "Sanctuary State" California. Immigrants who break the law and enter the country illegally and thieves who shoplift or loot up to $1,000 worth of merchandise per store can do so with impunity.

In other words, there are no consequences.

But if I sleep in my car in a public place, I can be arrested and go to jail.

Before so many communities in Orange County, California passed ordinances making it unlawful to sleep in one's car at night on a city street, there were options. Find a quiet, isolated neighborhood to park in, put up the blinders to cover the front windows, and settle in. Walmart used to allow overnight parking in distant parts of its immense parking lots after 8pm. When Walmart was open 24-hours, a person could use the restroom for an overnight emergency. Predictably, this resulted in homeless individuals forming "night camps" from their cars and look after each other. This was a lot safer than being in one of the public shelters with drug addicts, sex predators, or mentally troubled individuals. I heard many stories of victims being knifed and attacked over little or no change in their pockets.

Unfortunately, Walmart acquiesced to local ordinances and political pressure and put a stop to ALL overnight parking.

So what did I do when Nature called and I regretted drinking that Big Gulp from 7-11?

A bit of planning is in order. I made mental notes of restaurants who were open all night, gyms that were open 24 hours, and 24-hour gas stations.

Denny's To The Rescue

If there is an all-night diner in your neighborhood, you may be in luck. Denny's is a good choice if you are willing to flip your sleep time and don't mind buying some coffee and toast and sit at the counter. Smile and be friendly. Some waitresses/waiters will let you occupy a booth or table. Don't forget your appearance and good hygiene. If you look homeless and smell like ripe garlic, you will not be welcomed.

Because Denny's is open 24-7, I thought it was a good place to park at night—until I realized it is also a favorite hangout for sheriffs and police. You don't want them shining a flashlight in your face at 1 a.m. while you are asleep in your car in the parking lot. If you find yourself in that situation, simply explain you were tired from driving and pulled over to take a quick nap.

Another option is going to a campground and renting a space where you can pitch a tent. I never did that, but I met a woman my age who lived that way for many months. She stayed at a lesser-known campsite and rented a space that was close to the bathrooms and showers. She had purchased a good-sized tent, a comfortable sleeping bag and air mattress. She said it was just like being on vacation!

Almost.

She did well until her car with only a few more payments remaining got repossessed. Then the cold, wet winter months arrived. She eventually went to live with her son in another country and started a fresh new life.

The YMCA

If you do not shower or bathe after a few days, especially during the summer months, you will feel and smell like a very ripe onion. Or worse.

Steve Harvey once described how he would go to the men's room in an upscale Hollywood hotel early in the morning and bathe using paper towels, soap, and water. As long as he was early enough and did not attract attention from the staff or patrons, his scheme worked for him for many months. He did this until he got his big break in television. He, too, was living out of his car.

So, what are your options?

If you have family or friends who will let you bathe or shower in their home, kiss the ground they stand on.

They may not be up to having you live in their home, but a hot shower with soap and shampoo will feel like a king's ransom!

Some gyms have private showers, but you will need to be a member. I got around this by asking for a FREE trial membership, usually 14 days. I ended up going to many different gyms, but I found out which ones were clean and which ones weren't. If you are eligible for Medicare, the Silver Sneakers program is free. Not all gyms are equal, so if you have to pay to use their facilities, make sure they are clean and can accommodate your needs.

(Hygiene Tip: Always have a pair of inexpensive flip flops to wear in public showers.)

A case in point was the YMCA in Mission Viejo. It was my lifeline for three years. I qualified for a reduced membership fee to use their showers, especially the larger, roomier accessible stalls with the largest walk space to set aside my clothing and towels.

The only problems I ever experienced were when the city would shut off the water—unannounced and with no advance warning. Another time, someone on staff turned down the water heater thermostat during the Christmas holiday season. The water barely got above tepid. This was not fun during the cold winter months, but for every time I could shower and wash my hair, I still felt incredibly grateful.

YMCA facilities are everywhere. They are a Christian organization and are an invaluable resource for other services.

Everyone Is Entitled To A Bad Day

The only time I ever experienced any kind of disrespect because of my homeless status occurred when a young, over-zealous desk clerk yelled at me in front of a group of members in the lobby of a different YMCA location. Unbeknownst to me, my membership had lapsed and my account was past due. I remained calm and tried to explain I didn't have internet and couldn't receive any electronic messages. He continued to yell at me in front of everyone until the Director, Jennifer Heinen, came out of her office, took me aside and showed me on her computer what the problem was. I had no clue, but she kindly worked out everything with me and got me back in good standing.

It was a long time before I returned to that location, but in fact, it became my favorite gym to go to everyday for many years. I loved the classes for older adults and found the staff to be friendly, dedicated, and professional.

I can only assume the desk clerk who became so irate with me had personal issues going on that day. It can happen to any of us.

Public Libraries

Sad to say, public libraries aren't what they used to be.

When I was just starting school, my mother would take me to the library, and I would check out 12-14 books at a time. When I was in middle school, I lived close to a very small but quaint library that I would walk to on Saturdays and pick out a book to read until it was time for the library to close. And when I was in high school and could drive, I would go to the city library during the summer months and read everything I could on a particular subject. One summer it was the history of China. The next summer it was the history of Japan. I felt as if the Universe was at my fingertips!

Even as an adult, I have always found most public libraries a favorite place to "hang out." Free parking, free access to the Internet, books, magazines, newspapers, and very clean restrooms!

Such a deal!

Unfortunately, the unruly and unwashed population has also discovered the positive advantages of public libraries. Some libraries in Orange County's wealthiest communities are overrun with drug addicts, alcoholics, and other troubled individuals who cannot hold a job and have no place to go during the day. Some locations have turned into daycare centers for rowdy school children to be at while they wait until their working parents can pick them up.

Forget about the "Silence is golden" rule and authority of Marion the Librarian. I have witnessed several men sitting in the computer section shouting, talking loudly across the room until some timid librarian comes over to meekly ask them to keep their voices down—for the umpteenth time THAT hour. These individuals, most of them homeless, are not there to use the resources to find a job or research social services that could help them. They are there to be with their buddies until they can return to the shelters and half-way houses. I have walked into some library restrooms to find somebody washing her hair or laundry in the water basin. During the pandemic, few if any public libraries were open past 5pm or available seven days a week.

Not all libraries have this problem. Know which ones are clean and well supervised. I still love working in the library, but I bring sanitizer and Lysol towels to clean the work area thoroughly.

One of my favorite libraries is the municipal library of Mission Viejo: spacious and clean, with worktables that are occupied quickly. My favorite spot is the Heritage Room, with its large fireplace, enormous leather chairs and limited seating. It is an inviting refuge during rainstorms and cold winter months. I would settle in with my cup of coffee, enjoy the fireplace, watch the weather from inside and quietly read until closing time.

One November, I learned the hard way about the need to sanitize or clean any surfaces in public places. I picked up a virus somewhere between this library and the showers at the YMCA. The virus developed into a serious case of bronchitis that relapsed twice and lasted two months. My long-suffering roommates at the time had to put up with my all-night coughing spasms. They never mentioned a thing to me. I'm sure their patience was tested, but their angel wings have grown!

Forewarned is Forearmed

As I have stated previously, we don't make the best choices when we are under stress.

When we enter survival mode, we need to have taken the time to think BEFORE a bad situation happens.

In addition to restaurants, gyms and safe places to be at, what other resources can you reach out to? What friends and family are willing to help out, and to what extent? Do you belong to a group, organization, or church that might offer assistance? I know of one Christian church which, due to its size and vast resources, was able to find temporary housing for a few of its homeless congregants until they were able to get jobs and support themselves. Mormon churches are legendary when it comes to meeting the needs of their congregants.

Last Words Of Advice

- Keep your expectations reasonable.
- Don't allow any setbacks or rejections to cause you to become bitter or victimized.
- Nobody likes a sourpuss, let alone help one.
- Be grateful and humble towards any offer of help, no matter how small.
- And don't give up. If the only thing you do on any day is put one foot in front of the other, that is progress.

RECOMMENDED

Books

Peace from Broken Pieces (2012) by Iyanla Van Zant

You Can Heal Your Life (1984) by Louise Hay

Peace and Plenty (2010) by Sarah Ban Breathnach

Outrageous Openness: Letting the Divine Take the Lead (2014) by Tosha Silver

Further Research

Homelessness in Orange County: The Costs to Our Community (2018) Unitedwayoc.org/resources

Unitedtoendhomelessness.org

Music

"In the Land of I AM" (2000), CD, Rickie Byars

"Glorious!" The Agape International Choir (2016), CD, Rickie Byars

"Soul Fulfilling with Rickie Byars" Wednesday Evening Meet-Up on YouTube

ABOUT THE AUTHOR

California native Cheryl Cuttineau wrote her first book when she was 19. A budding Renaissance woman, she didn't limit her interests to writing: Travel Agent, World traveler, Musician, public school Educator, Polyglot(French, German and Italian), Sales & Marketing Account Executive, Copywriter, Grant Writer and Reviewer, Legal Administrator, Hypnotherapist, Grief Counselor, Fundraiser, Reiki Healer, Holistic Health Coach, Shaman Practitioner, Animal Empath, Animal Rescue Activist, Entrepreneur, Vedic Astrologer, Philanthropist, Co- Director of the Little Buffalo Foundation, and current Director of the future Abundant Good Trust Foundation.

As a result of her Catholic upbringing, Cheryl has always had an interest in spirituality and mysticism. She was also influenced by her paternal grandmother, who was an Astrologer and member of the Rosicrucians and Theosophical societies. Her Aunt, a Zen teacher, introduced her to the Vedic system of Astrology.

On track to enroll at UC Davis as a pre-med veterinary student, the first of two life-changing events intervened to alter the course of her life. When Cheryl was

19, her mother surrendered to an eight-year battle with breast and bone cancer.

The second event is the subject of this book.

Today Cheryl is living her best life. She spends her time volunteering at the local cat sanctuary in Laguna Beach, going to the gym, growing her own vegetables, and writing her next books, *Cancer: The Sacred Journey,* and *The Soul Doesn't Come Here to Retire.*

If you want to be notified when either of these books is published, send your full name and email address to:

cherylc@tutamail.com

www.ingramcontent.com/pod-product-compliance
Lightning Source LLC
LaVergne TN
LVHW012113160826
845678LV00014B/3071

* 9 7 8 1 8 3 5 5 6 1 9 3 5 *